craft smart

JEWELLERY

Laura Torres

QED Project Editor: Ruth Symons

Created for QED Publishing by Tall Tree Ltd
Editor: Catherine Saunders
Designers: Jonathan Vipond and Marisa Renzullo
Illustrator: Geraint Ford
Photography: Michael Wicks

First published in the UK in 2013 by
QED Publishing, a Quarto Group company
6 Blundell Street
London N7 9BH

www.qed-publishing.co.uk

A catalogue record for this book is available from the British Library.

ISBN 978 1 78171 099 9

Printed in China

Picture credits
(t=top, b=bottom, l=left, r=right, c=centre, fc=front cover, bc=back cover)
Shutterstock Africa Studio, 5tr, 8r; Alexander Gospodinov, fcl, bccl;
Bennyartist, fcc, bcc, 3tr, 9, 11, 13, 15, 17, 19, 21, 23, 25, 27, 29, 31; CLM,
12tr; Coprid, 3br; cosma, 3bl; cristi180884, 4r; Diana Taliun, 10bl;
dogboxstudio, 20tr; Dulce Rubia, 3b; Feng Yu, 3r, 5l; Garsya, fccl; Iakov
Filimonov, 10r, 22tr; Ilya Akinshin, 14l; jabiru, fccr; jeka84, 3bl, 19tr; Jim
Hughes, 3tl, 4tr, 28tr; kuma, 20tl, bl; Madlen, 3l, tr, r, 18t; magicoven, 5b;
MaPaSa, fcr, bctr; Nattika, fcl, bccl, 4br; Noraluca013, fcc, bctr; oksix, 4l;
optimarc, fcc, bct; pukach, fcl; Tatiana Volgutova, 16r; Tomas Jasinskis, 3r;
Vaclav Mach, 5r.

Note to Adults:
Some children might be able to
do some or all of these projects
on their own, while others might
need more help. These are
projects that you can work on
together, not only to avoid any
problems or accidents, but also
to share in the fun of making crafts.

In preparation of this book, all due
care has been exercised with regard
to the activities and advice
depicted. The publishers regret that
they can accept no liability for any
loss or injury sustained.

At the top of the page for each project you will
find this handy key. It will tell you the difficulty
level to expect from each project:

Quick creative fix
These projects are quick, easy and
perfect for a beginner.

Sharpen your skills
Confident with your beginner skills? Move onto
these slightly tougher projects.

Ready for a challenge
For a challenging project you can really
get stuck into.

Creative masterpiece
Think you can tackle the toughest craft
projects? Have a go at these.

CONTENTS

MATERIALS

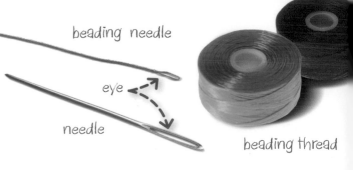

beading needle

eye

needle

beading thread

Beads, beading thread, clasps, chain and wire are sold in craft shops, department stores and online. You can also visit speciality bead shops for a huge range of colours and styles.

Découpage glue

You can purchase pre-made découpage glue. You can also make your own by mixing two parts of PVA glue to one part water.

seed beads

Seed beads

These small beads come in varying sizes – the higher the number, the smaller the bead. You can use any size for the projects in this book, but larger sizes are easier to work with. Make sure that your needle has a small enough eye for the beads to slide over.

Beading thread and beading elastic

Beading thread is stronger than ordinary thread. Beading elastic is a thin stretchy cord.

Beading needle

Beading needles are made of a strong, flexible wire so that beads can pass easily over the eye. You can use a regular needle if the eye is small enough for the beads to pass over.

Jump ring

A jump ring is a metal loop that you can open to put on beads or charms.

jump rings

skein of embroidery thread

crochet hooks

Cord

There are many types of cord available. You can purchase leather, or a less expensive cord that looks like leather, in a variety of colours.

ball chain

Ball chain

This inexpensive chain is made up of little metal balls. It is easy to cut to the correct length with scissors or nail clippers and is sold with clasps. Ball chains also come in a variety of colours.

Embroidery thread

There are two kinds of embroidery thread, one with strands that you can separate, and one that you can't separate. Either kind is fine for friendship bracelets, but always use the same kind in any single bracelet.

Glue

Any kind of glue that dries clear (PVA is a good choice) can be used to dab onto knots in thread to stop them from unravelling.

Crochet hook

Crochet hooks come in different sizes. It is important to use the hook size given in the project instructions if you can, but it is OK to substitute a hook that is one size above or below.

Jewellery clasps

You will find a wide variety of clasps wherever jewellery supplies are sold. Choose one that will look good with your project and is easy to open and close.

jewellery clasps

Wire

Wire comes in different gauges. The higher the number of the gauge, the thinner the wire, and the more flexible it is.

wire

PVA glue

TECHNIQUES

DÉCOUPAGE

Découpage is the art of gluing bits of paper or fabric onto an object. You can use this technique to make beads (see pages **14-15**) or other art and craft projects.

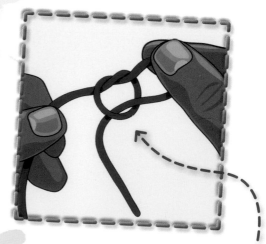

CROCHET TIPS

Here are some tips to help you with the projects on pages 24 – 27. It is a good idea to practise your crochet technique before you begin these crafts.

Slip Knot

1 Crocheting starts with a slip knot. Make a loop near the end of the thread.

2 Make another loop in the tail end of the wool and push it through the first loop. Pull tight.

Keeping tension in the wool

Hold the crochet hook in your writing hand. Hold the wool in your other hand and use your index finger to keep the wool tight.

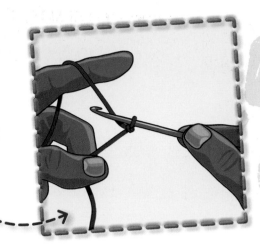

Creating new rows

To create the first row, see page 24 for instructions.

1 To start the second row, stick the crochet hook in the second loop from the hook, hook the wool and bring it through just the first loop. You will now have two loops on the crochet hook.

2 Hook the wool again and bring it through both loops. Repeat the process to the end of the chain.

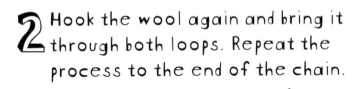

3 For the third row, insert the hook through the top two loops, then work as steps 1 and 2, pulling the wool through one and then both loops. Use this method to crochet as many rows as you want.

FRIENDSHIP BRACELET

Friendship bracelets are fun to make, and to share. This diagonal stripe pattern is a classic.

YOU WILL NEED:

- Three colours of embroidery thread
- Scissors
- Sticky tape

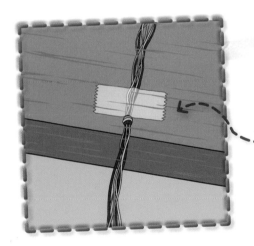

1 Cut two 30 cm pieces of each colour of embroidery thread. Gather the six strands together and tie a knot at the top, leaving a 10 cm tail. Tape the thread down, just above the knot.

2 Sort the strands by colour. Take the first strand and loop it over the second strand, so it looks like a '4'. Take the first strand underneath the second strand and through the loop.

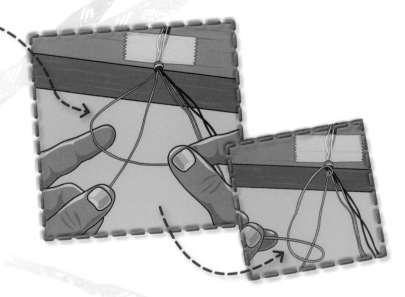

3 You should now have a knot. Hold the second strand straight and taut while you tighten the knot. Repeat step 2 to make a second knot on the same strand. You have now made a double knot.

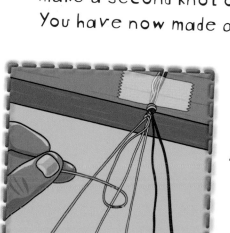

4 With the same thread, double knot around each of the remaining strands, just as you did in steps 2 and 3. Go from left to right, holding the strands straight and tight as you knot.

5 You should now have a different thread on the far left. Repeat steps 2, 3 and 4. Keep going until the bracelet is as long as you want. Tie a knot with all the strands at the end of the bracelet.

Give a friendship bracelet to each of your best friends to show how much you care.

WRAP FRIENDSHIP BRACELET

This colourful knotted bracelet looks great wrapped around your wrist several times.

YOU WILL NEED:

- Three different colours of embroidery thread, 1-2 metres long
- Sticky tape
- Scissors

1 Tie a knot at the top of the three lengths of thread, leaving 10 cm of thread above the knot. Tape the thread down, just above the knot. Pull one strand to the left of the other two.

2 Take the left strand and loop it over the other strands, so it looks like a '4'. Take the strand underneath the others and through the loop. This will form a knot.

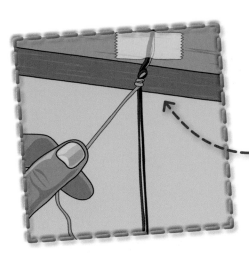

3 Hold the two other strands straight and tighten the knot. Repeat step 2 until you want to change colours.

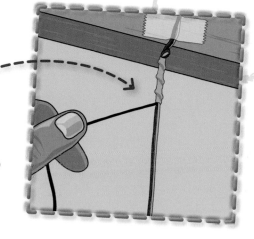

4 To change colours, pull a different coloured strand out to the left. Repeat steps 2 and 3.

5 When the bracelet is long enough, tie a knot at the end. Trim the tails at both ends so they are just long enough to tie the bracelet together.

Experiment with different colours. Try four or five colours when you have mastered three.

FRIENDSHIP BEADS

YOU WILL NEED:

- Bead with wide hole
- Darning needle
- Embroidery thread
- Glue
- Scissors

You can string these colourful beads together to make bracelets or necklaces, or swap them with your friends.

1 Cut a piece of thread about 1 m long. Thread it through the bead and tie a knot around the bead. Trim the short end of the thread.

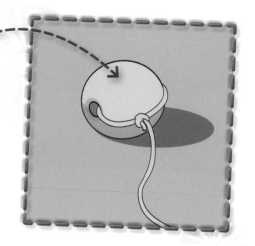

2 Put a dab of glue on the knot. Turn the thread so the knot is inside the bead. Leave to dry.

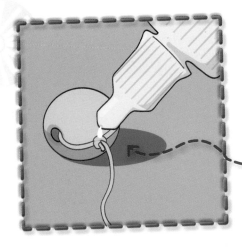

3 Using the needle, take the thread around the bead and through the hole. Pull the thread tight.

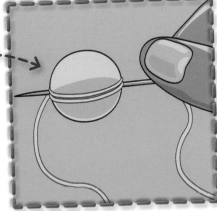

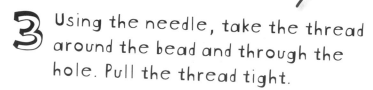

4 Repeat step 3 until the bead is covered. Pull the thread tight every time.

5 Knot the thread at the top of the bead and pull tight. Trim the thread and put a dab of glue on the knot. Use the needle to push the knot inside the bead.

Use the same method if you want to layer another colour on top. To make a striped bead, thread two colours of thread onto the same needle and follow the steps.

DÉCOUPAGE NECKLACE

This is a fun way to turn scraps of fabric into a wearable work of art.

YOU WILL NEED:

- A selection of fabric scraps
- 10 large wooden beads
- Scissors
- Découpage glue (see page 4)
- Paintbrush
- Skewer
- Bowl

1 Cut a scrap of fabric that fits halfway around a bead and then cut it into smaller strips. Thread a bead onto a skewer.

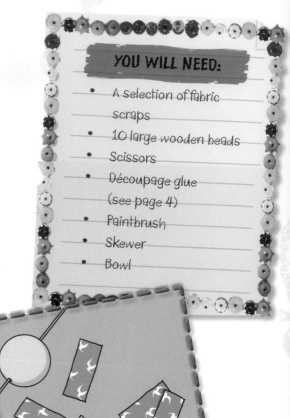

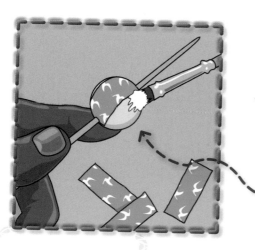

2 Dab some glue onto the bead and smooth on a fabric strip. Add some more glue to the bead. Smooth on another strip, overlapping the first one. Continue adding strips until half the bead is covered.

3 Paint glue over the covered part of the bead and rest the skewer over a bowl to let the bead dry. Repeat step 2 to cover the second half of the bead. Follow steps 1, 2 and 3 to cover ten beads. Leave the beads to dry.

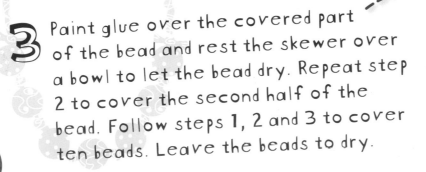

4 Cut a strip of fabric 1 cm wide and 1 m long. Cut one end at an angle. Thread on the beads, knotting the fabric in between each bead.

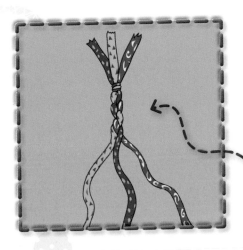

5 Cut six strips of fabric about 40 cm long. Make two plaits and knot the ends. Tie them to the ends of the necklace and knot together.

If you make a few extra beads, you can create a matching bracelet. Instead of knotting between each découpage bead, try adding a smaller wooden bead.

WOVEN BEAD BRACELET

Turn an ordinary hair comb into a loom to make these woven bracelets. You can use different colour combinations to make unique designs.

YOU WILL NEED:

- Three 65 cm-long pieces of embroidery thread
- One 1 m piece of beading thread
- Beading needle
- Seed beads
- Comb
- Sticky tape
- Scissors

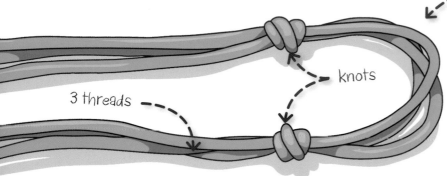

knots

3 threads

1 Hold the three pieces of embroidery thread together. Find the centre point of the thread and tie a knot on each side, 2 cm from the centre.

2 Tape the comb to the edge of a table with the teeth sticking up. Place the knots behind the comb and tape down the thread loop. Separate the six pieces of thread and slip them through the teeth of the comb.

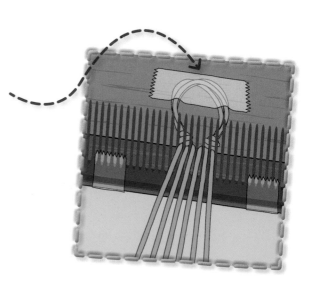

3 Thread the beading thread onto the needle and tie a knot at the end. Take the needle through the left knot. Thread five seed beads onto the needle.

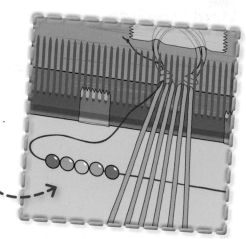

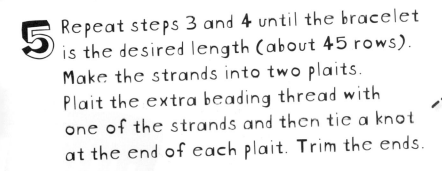

4 Pass the needle underneath the strands of thread. Push the beads up between the strands with your finger. Pass the needle over the top of the strands and through the beads in the **opposite** direction.

5 Repeat steps 3 and **4** until the bracelet is the desired length (about **45 rows**). Make the strands into two plaits. Plait the extra beading thread with one of the strands and then tie a knot at the end of each plait. Trim the ends.

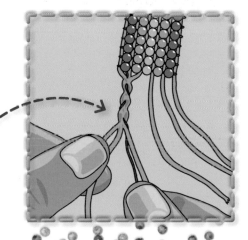

Weave double the number of rows to make a dramatic choker-style necklace.

PRETTY PIN BROOCH

This brooch is simple yet stylish. Wear one on its own or create a few to wear together.

YOU WILL NEED:

- Safety pin
- 24 or 28 gauge wire
- About 20 seed beads and some larger beads
- Large jump ring
- Wire clippers or fingernail clippers

1 Cut a piece of wire about 20 cm long. Twist one end of the wire around the bottom of the safety pin two or three times.

2 Thread three or four seed beads onto the wire. On the side of the pin that does not open, wind the wire around twice to keep the beads in place.

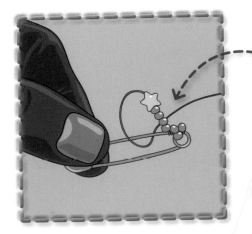

3 Continue threading more beads, adding some larger beads as well. Wind the wire around the pin after every three or four beads.

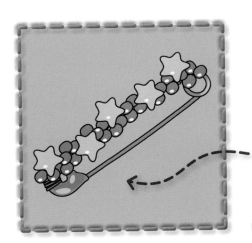

4 When you get to the end of the pin, wind the wire around it three times to secure it. Cut the wire close to the pin.

5 Open the jump ring and thread on some beads. Thread the jump ring through the bottom loop of the safety pin and close it.

Experiment with different coloured beads to match your favourite outfits. These brooches make great gifts, too!

FLOWER POWER HAIRBAND

You'll never have another bad hair day with this colourful hair accessory.

YOU WILL NEED:

- Felt
- Pen
- Ruler
- Scissors
- Needle
- Thread
- Cotton wool ball
- Bead
- Hairband

1 Draw a circle on the felt about 6 cm wide and cut it out. Cut four 1.5 cm slits into the circle, equal distances apart.

2 Cut four more slits between the first four to make eight equal-sized petals. Cut each petal so it forms a half circle on one side.

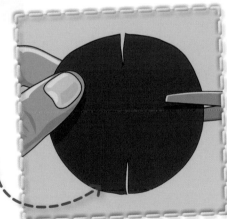

3 Thread the needle and knot the end. Take the needle through the tip of each petal, coming from the inside of the flower each time.

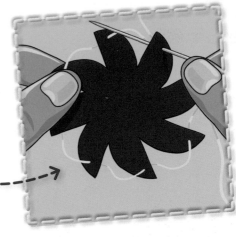

4 Go through the first petal again to complete the circle. Put a cotton wool ball in the centre of the flower. Pull the thread tight so the circle is closed. Make a stitch and knot the thread.

5 Thread on a bead and sew it onto the fabric. Take the needle through to the back of the flower and sew on a hairband. Tie a knot and trim the thread.

There are lots of ways to use these felt flowers. You could make a brooch or sew a flower onto the headband from page 24.

TWISTED BRACELET

Turn a simple ball chain into something special with some cord and embroidery thread. Two or three of these bracelets look great on your wrist.

YOU WILL NEED:
- Ball chain with clasp
- Scissors
- Leather or cotton cord
- Embroidery thread
- Glue

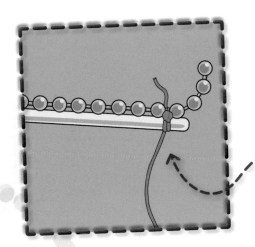

1 Take the end of the chain without the clasp and cut it to fit your wrist. Cut the cord about 2 cm shorter than the chain and cut the embroidery thread to four times the length of the cord. Use the thread to tie the chain and the cord together, leaving two or three chain links at the end.

2 Put a dab of glue on the knot. Wrap the thread tightly around the cord, chain and tail of the thread.

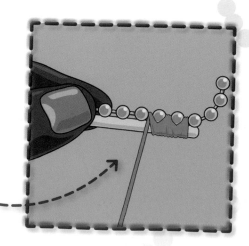

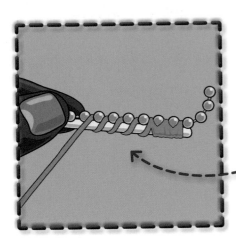

3 Wrap the thread around the chain and cord, going in between each link of the chain. As you do this, the chain will naturally twist around the cord.

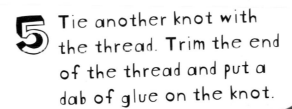

4 When you get to the clasp end, tie the thread in a knot. Wrap the thread around a few times to secure everything in place.

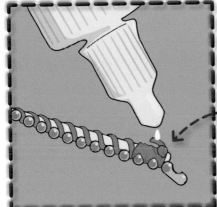

5 Tie another knot with the thread. Trim the end of the thread and put a dab of glue on the knot.

You can use the same method to make a necklace. Tape one end of the chain to a table to make wrapping the longer length easier.

CROCHET HEADBAND

Crochet these thick or thin, in any colour. Tie one around your head for a hippy chick look.

YOU WILL NEED:
- Wool
- Size 4 mm crochet hook (UK size 8, US size 6)
- Scissors

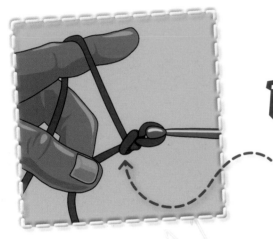

1 Make a slip knot (see page 6) in the wool, leaving a 15 cm tail. Insert the crochet hook and tighten the knot until it is slightly loose around the hook. Keeping tension (see page 7), hook the wool and bring it through the loop.

2 You will now have a new loop on the crochet hook. Repeat step 1 until the row of stitches is almost long enough to fit around your head.

3 Start a new row (see steps 1 and 2 on page 7). Repeat to the end of the chain.

4 Crochet as many rows as you need (see page 7). Cut the wool, leaving a 15 cm tail. Remove the crochet hook and pull the wool through the remaining loop.

5 Trim the wool on both ends of the headband so they are even. Use the wool ends to tie the headband in place.

Use multi-coloured wool for a rainbow effect or add a felt flower from page 21.

STRETCHY RINGS

Once you master a single crochet stitch, you'll be hooked on making these stretchy, colourful rings.

YOU WILL NEED:

- Thin beading elastic
- Size 1.5 mm crochet hook (UK size 2, US size 7)
- Glue
- Scissors

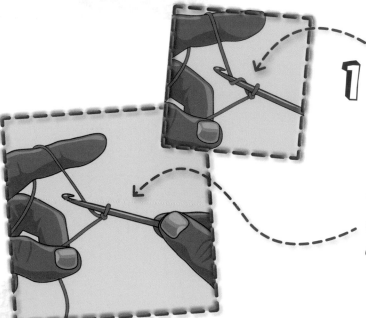

1 Make a slip knot in the cord (see page 6), leaving a 4 cm tail. Insert the crochet hook and tighten the knot until it is only slightly loose. Keeping tension on the elastic cord (see page 7), hook the cord and bring it through the loop.

2 You will now have a new loop on the crochet hook. Repeat step 1 until the row of stitches is long enough to go around your finger.

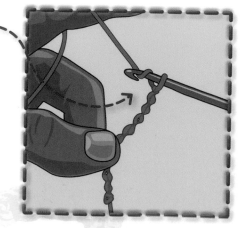

3 Stick the crochet hook through the first loop. Hook the cord and bring it through both loops to make a circle.

4 Stick the crochet hook in the second loop and bring it through just the first loop (you will now have two loops on the hook). Hook the cord again and bring it through both loops. Repeat all the way around the ring. Add at least 2 rows.

5 After the last stitch, cut the cord, leaving a **4 cm** tail. Pull it through the loop on your crochet hook. Remove the hook and tie the two ends together on the inside of the ring. Put a dab of glue on the knot and trim the ends.

You can choose how thick or thin your ring is by adding as many rows as you want.

TRIPLE STRAND BRACELET

You'll want to wear this pretty bracelet every day. Why not make one to match all your favourite outfits?

YOU WILL NEED:

- Beading thread
- Beading needle
- A clasp
- Seed beads
- Other small beads
- Sticky tape
- Glue
- Scissors

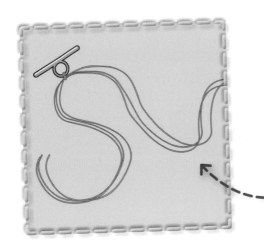

1 Cut three 50 cm pieces of thread. Hold the strands together and thread them through one end of the clasp. Leave a 12 cm tail and knot the thread around the clasp.

2 Thread the beading needle onto one of the long strands of thread. Use the needle to thread on seed beads until the bracelet is as long as you want. Take off the needle and put a piece of tape around the thread to hold the beads in place.

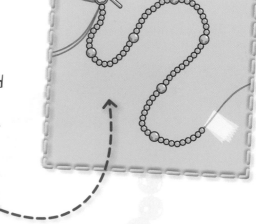

28

3 Repeat step 2 with the other two strands, making sure that they are all the same length. Take the tape off the strands and gather them together.

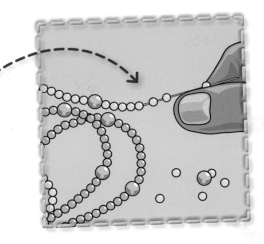

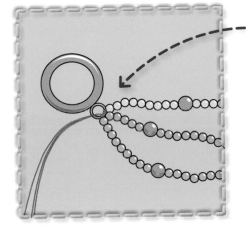

4 Thread all three strands onto the needle. Take the needle through the other end of the clasp twice and pull it tight.

5 Thread the needle through three seed beads on one strand. Tie a knot between the beads. Dab some glue on the knot and trim the ends of the thread. Repeat on the other end of the bracelet.

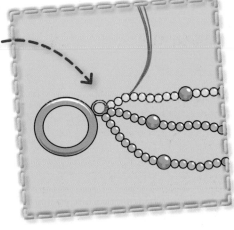

Try mixing in silver beads with the seed beads for extra sparkle.

DAISY CHAIN NECKLACE

Use seed beads to make a daisy chain you can keep forever.

YOU WILL NEED:

- Seed beads in three colours
- A clasp
- Beading thread
- Beading needle
- Scissors
- Glue

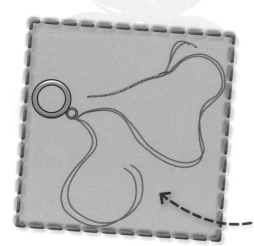

1 Cut a piece of beading thread four times the length you want your necklace to be. Double-thread the needle and pull it to the centre of the thread. Tie the two ends of the thread around one side of the clasp, leaving a 10 cm tail.

2 String ten seed beads onto the thread. Then string six more beads in the colour you want your flower to be. Bring the needle back up through the first flower bead. Pull the thread to make a circle.

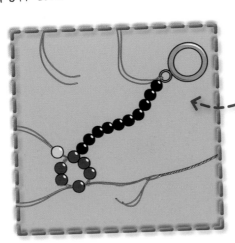

3 String on one bead in another colour to make the centre of the flower. Take the needle through the fourth flower bead. Pull tight.

30

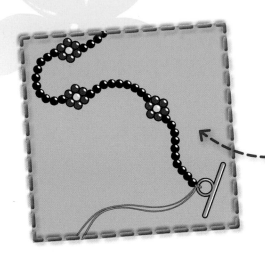

4 Repeat steps 2 and 3 until your necklace is the desired length. Take the needle through the other side of the clasp twice. Pull tight.

5 Take the needle through three beads. Tie a knot between the beads. Put a dab of glue on the knot and trim the ends of the thread. Repeat on the other end of the necklace.

Create a shorter chain to to make a daisy chain bracelet.

INDEX